FRANK RODGERS'
DERBYSHIRE

FRANK RODGERS'
DERBYSHIRE

Breedon Books
Publishing Company
Derby

First published in Great Britain by
The Breedon Books Publishing Company Limited
44 Friar Gate, Derby, DE1 1DA.
1994

ISBN 1 873626 79 7

Printed and bound by Butler & Tanner, Frome & London.
Covers printed by BDC Printing Services Limited of Derby

Contents

Dedication

This book is dedicated to my wife, Dorothy, and our sons, Chris and Martin.

Acknowledgements

My thanks go to John Heath for checking my captions and his kind 'potted history' of me in the Introduction, and to Roy Deeley for his help in printing many of the photographs from my original negatives. I also thank my son Chris for his helpful suggestions in the compilation of this book.

Introduction

BORN into a Derbyshire farming family at Weston Underwood, Frank Rodgers grew up in the South Derbyshire countryside, absorbing the natural and physical world, and from Weston Underwood he frequently visited his grandfather's farm — Red Mire Gap — at Hulland Ward.

From an early age he recorded, in pencil sketches and in water colours, the natural scene and was an admirer of the work of Sir William Russell Flint. He won a scholarship to the Derby School of Art at the age of 14, but, of course, it was essential that he should begin earning a living, which he did by becoming an apprentice at International Combustion Limited in the pattern-making shop.

He found satisfaction in working with wood and developed this interest by returning to the Derby School of Art in Green Lane to attend woodwork and wood-carving classes. There he also attended classes in painting, particularly in water colours. In retrospect, he wishes that he had followed this interest, but instead he took up photography and with his innate feeling for composition he was to explore this world for the rest of his life.

Frank's first camera was a folding Coronet which cost 15s (75p) in 1932. He progressed from this one-stop, one-speed piece of photographic equipment to a four-guinea Agfa Speedex which had a variety of stops and speeds and later to a Zeiss Ikon Super-Ikonta. As a member of the Derby Photographic Society, he exhibited at the annual shows in Derby Museum's Art Gallery and success came his way in 1940, when he won a Kodak competition with his Super-Ikonta.

Many of the photographs included in this book have an historical significance, as well as artistic merit, for when he began his photographic career, Frank had few thoughts about publishing his efforts. One week, however, he submitted three examples of his work to the *Manchester Guardian* with a covering letter pointing

A carved wooden figure which Frank did as a young man. It is based on his father, who Frank made into a sailor in this work.

out that pictures of Derbyshire never appeared in their pages. The following week the three pictures were published, and one was even used on the cover of the *Manchester Guardian Weekly*. Encouraged by this, Frank continued to send in photographs which were used regularly.

During the war, when he was in a reserved occupation, he joined a Home Guard ack-ack unit and also a fire-fighting team and so there was little time for other activities, but peace was restored he resumed his photographic career in earnest and since then many of his photographs have been published in a variety of journals, sometimes with an accompany-

Frank Rodgers, camera in hand. ROY DEELEY

A watercolour painted by Frank Rodgers when he was in his 20s.

ing article, as well as in guide books and calendars.

For several years a landscape series appeared in the *Staffordshire Advertiser* and he also contributed to the *Derbyshire Advertiser*. Since 1940 he has been a regular contributor to the *Derbyshire Life and Countryside* in which his collaboration with Roy Christian on 'Derbyshire Villages' is an on-going saga which began in 1980, although his association with Roy's publications began in 1961. More recently he has contributed a series of walks which are based on his exploration of the county scene, always accompanied by his wife, Dorothy, whom he first met in 1934, married in 1938, and with whom he shares his working retirement at their cottage in Holloway, where they overlook their beloved hills, woods and fields.

In 1950, Frank joined Rolls-Royce Ltd in their model-making department, constructing models in wood and perspex for aero test-rigs. This, allied with his photographic skills, led to him being transferred to the Exhibition Department where he was a member of a design team which set-up exhibitions at home and overseas. Rolls Royce's merger with Bristol Aircraft and the collapse of the company in 1971 left him redundant, but at the age of 58 he became a technician on the staff of the Derby and District College of Technology, so resuming a link with an institution, then on Normanton Road, in which he had been a part-time lecturer during and after World War Two.

His first publication was *Derby Old and New* which has been recently revised. Pictures from this book were shown on television, as was a programme he researched, on lead-mining in Derbyshire. More recently has seen the production of a new edition of his *Curiosities of the Peak District*.

Although not as spritely as of yesteryear, this gentle, amiable octogenerian can still be seen somewhere in Derbyshire, accompanied by Dorothy, capturing that special scene with his Rolleicord and Olympus cameras. The resulting photographs are the hall-mark of a person with a love of the countryside and a keen eye to record it.

John Heath
October 1994

Walk on a Spring Day in 1939

It is now 60 years since I met my wife Dorothy, and during that time we have explored the hills and dales of Derbyshire, later to be joined by our sons Chris and Martin. There have been many memorable days and one of the most outstanding – and certainly the most significant and successful photographically – was in the spring of 1939. In glorious sunshine, my wife and I alighted from the bus in Ashbourne, our intended route being through the very attractive village of Tissington and the return down picturesque Dovedale. I had always carried my camera and had just acquired a Zeiss Ikon Super Ikonta. On that day I took 25 photographs and through the years they have all been published, many in the old *Manchester Guardian*, on calendars and on the covers of the *Country Life*, *The Lady* and other national magazines together with our own *Derbyshire Countryside*, as it was then called.

The Hall in Fenny Bentley, home of the Beresford family in the fifteenth century, is an ancient manor fortified by a medieval tower and makes a pleasant picture seen from the main road.

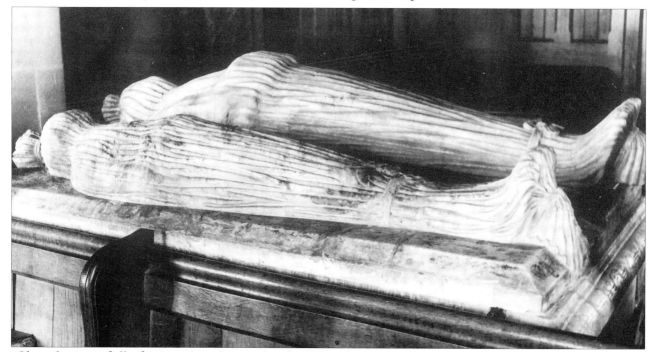

Churches are full of interest and records of village characters. The church at Fenny Bentley has a remarkable tomb of the Beresfords, with Thomas and his wife Agnes represented as tied up in shrouds. Their 21 children are shown in a similar fashion around the sides of the tomb but are unfortunately obscured by a seat.

Close by the tomb is a finely-carved screen dating from the fifteenth century.

The Hall's orchard with lambs sheltering beneath fruit trees in full bloom epitomises spring.

Cottages and a small bridge over the Bentley Brook makes a pleasant scene and my wife completes the picture.

Photographs taken against the light have a particular quality and this scene, with the sun shining through the leaves of a beech tree, caught my eye as we climbed the hill towards Tissington.

Tissington village is full of pictures but we had a long walk ahead. A fine line of beeches backed the pond and the title 'Spring Comes to the Beeches' came to mind as I took this view. The editor of *Country Life* used this title when he carried the picture on the cover of the magazine and it has appeared on calendars and elsewhere many times since.

In this view across the pond I again felt a figure would improve the scene.

A splendid show of daffodils fronted the fine Elizabethan hall

The front gate to the Hall is a splendid example of the skill of Robert Bakewell, Derby's supreme craftsman in wrought iron work.

The road runs beside the river for about a mile down to the little hamlet of Milldale with lovely views like this one. Through the years this picture has been published many times and is still topical, for the charm of Mill Dale still remains. Perhaps it is not appreciated by the many motorists who have to keep their eyes on the road in the summer time today.

From Tissington a footpath crosses the fields to the River Dove and here we were suddenly confronted by a breathtaking view of Lode Mill in Mill Dale. This photograph also appeared on the cover of *Country Life* and has been published many times elsewhere.

We saw few motorists that day, and cows had been brought down to the river in the little hamlet beside Viator's Bridge.

The road leaves the dale in Milldale and we turned over this tiny packhorse bridge. Viator's Bridge is perhaps the most well-known among the many fine packhorse bridges in the county. Close by stood an old cornmill but this has now gone although one of its millstones lies in the river here.

The walk down Dovedale was sheer delight and the only people we saw until we reached the Stepping Stones were four fishermen, a lone walker, and a man with a donkey! Taken from the caves called Dove Holes, this view shows a modern Charles Cotton and Izaak Walton in close discussion as fishermen have done since the days of *The Compleat Angler*.

Close by a lone fisherman made a nice scene photographed against the light and was captioned 'Dovedale Fairyland' by one publisher.

Lower down the dale, Hurt's Wood, an ancient woodland, was carpeted with wild daffodils. Today they have all disappeared.

Also taken from Hurt's Wood, this picture was improved by the fisherman which made it saleable to *The Field* magazine who coloured it and used it on the cover.

A view which could be repeated many
times in the dale today – except for the
donkey. Donkey rides were given from
the Stepping Stones.

Lion's Head Rock is a well-known feature
in Dovedale and here we enlisted the help
of a lone walker to take this photograph
and include ourselves. Today a plaque set
in the rock records our debt to
F.A.Holmes MA JP of Buxton who did so
much to preserve this area for posterity.
He had the vision that Dovedale and the
Manifold Valley should become a National
Park and soon after these photographs
began to appear in the press he contacted
me to ask if I could help in his project.
This I was happy to do by contributing
articles and photographs to the press,
and our co-operation continued until his
death in 1947. The area was included in
the Peak District National Park created in
1951.

This unusual view of the dale is taken from Reynard's Cave which stands high on the Derbyshire side reached by a steep climb.

A few people give life to the famous Stepping Stones seen here from the flanks of Thorpe Cloud.

Taken from the same viewpoint as the previous picture, this view looking down river looks strangely bare, for today the river bank between river and road is clad with self-set trees.

From the Stepping Stones the footpath leads up Lin Dale to Thorpe village. Here for many years a Mrs Chadwick served teas, which were very popular with walkers and cyclists as can be seen here.

Another typical spring scene gave us our last picture before we turned towards Ashbourne, a walk of about 20 miles in all.

Derbyshire's Changing Scene

In photographing Derbyshire through the past 60 years there was never – mistakenly when seen in hindsight – any intention on my part to record scenes or features because they may change. They were taken as a matter of interest and love of the scene and a book of this kind was never in my mind! However, in the passing years many of my photographs have acquired a historical significance.

Like most large towns and cities, Derby has seen great changes. In the countryside the building of reservoirs has had the greatest impact on the landscape with several new ones having been constructed in recent times.

The pressure of modern traffic has resulted in the demolition of buildings in towns and villages. The photograph of Glenorchy Chapel at Cromford was taken to illustrate an article on George Newnes, the famous publisher who was born in the Manse, but both buildings have disappeared with the A6 road widening which included the opening of Scarthin Nick.

The tower windmills at Riddings, like so many relics of the industrial past, were demolished having outlived their usefulness. Similarly, many attractive old watermills have disappeared. Fortunately there are exceptions where they have been successfully converted into unusual dwellings. For instance, the bottle kiln at West Hallam has been incorporated into an attractive amenity.

Since World War Two, mechanisation has come to the farm, so that working horses are rarely seen and it is rare that milking time slows the village street to walking pace. The following photographs will revive memories of those more leisurely days.

In 1948, Derby Corporation published the first issue of *Spotlight on Derby* to which I was asked to contribute an illustrated article on the historical features which were then still standing in the town. This took the form of a walk which included 16 of the most interesting subjects, beginning with the old Derby School in St Peter's Churchyard and ending with the Old Mayor's Parlour in the Morledge. These photographs with their abridged captions will remind Derbeians of changes in the city and also what has been lost.

In Derby Town

Derby School in St Peter's Churchyard was built in 1554 when Queen Mary included a Free Grammar School among the services to be maintained by her large grants to the town. John Flamstead, the first Astronomer Royal, was educated here.

Becket Well stood in a small courtyard in Becket Well Lane and was one of several wells which supplied water to the town prior to 1700, when George Sorocold, the mill engineer, piped water from the Derwent into the streets.

The Old Silk Mill gates, seen here in the Wardwick, were made in about 1725 by Robert Bakewell, Derby's fine wrought-iron worker. They were made for the entrance to the Silk Mill beside the Derwent and were placed here in the Wardwick in 1920.

The Bonnie Prince Charlie
Room in Derby Museum has
the panelling from the room in
Exeter House where the fateful
decision was made to abandon
his march on London in 1745.

St Werburgh's Church, where Dr Johnson
was married, faces down The Wardwick and
here there is an unusual wrought-iron font
cover in the form of a crown, and a screen,
both by Bakewell.

This fine Jacobean House of 1611 faces the museum in the Wardwick.

The County Hall in St Mary's Gate was built in 1660 and is thought to be the setting for the trial of Hetty Sorrel in George Elliot's *Adam Bede*.

The Dolphin Inn of 1530 with a model dolphin as its sign.

The sixteenth-century tower of Derby Cathedral, seen here from St Mary's Gate, is claimed to be one of the finest examples of Gothic architecture in the country. The huge elaborate tomb of Bess of Hardwick, and another fine screen by Bakewell are to be seen in the church.

St Michael's Lane was an ancient cobbled
street with fine black and white timbered
cottages.

Lower down the lane this
prosaic building was the
first Methodist Preaching
House in Derby. In 1765,
John Wesley preached
here after a disorderly
crowd had prevented him
speaking in the Market
Place in the previous year.

The original Silk Mill building was built beside the River Derwent in 1718 by George Sorocold for the Lombe brothers and is claimed as the first factory in England. Robert Bakewell's gates, now in the Wardwick, stood between the brick pillars on the bridge which spanned the mill race.

The Chapel of St Mary's of the Bridge dates from the thirteenth century and is one of only a handful of bridge chapels still standing in England. The most tragic of the many events which have taken place here was the impaling of the heads of the Padley Martyrs in the time of Queen Mary.

The birthplace of Herbert Spencer, one of England's greatest philosophers, was commemorated on the white tablet on this house in Exeter Street.

This blacksmith's shop in Exeter Row stood not far from Herbert Spencer's birthplace – only a stone's throw from the Market Place.

Since *Spotlight on Derby* was published in 1948, a number of changes have taken place when the walk is repeated today. The old Derby School building in St Peter's Churchyard can no longer be seen from St Peter's Street, being hidden by a modern addition to St Peter's Church, while the well and cottages in Becket Well Lane disappeared when the Duckworth Square shopping centre was built in 1963. The Silk Mill Gates have been returned from the Wardwick to the Silk Mill site. Although externally the same, St Werburgh's Church is no longer a place of worship, at the present time housing the Cloisters Arcade Shopping Centre where Robert Bakewell's fine font cover may still be seen. Other large gates by Bakewell which at one time stood in St Mary's Gate now stand at the entrance to the Cathedral.

The old timbered buildings and the historic chapel in St Michael's Lane have been demolished, and the mill fleam of the Silk Mill, together with the bridge upon which the Bakewell gates stood, have disappeared. St Mary's Bridge and its chapel are unchanged but the tall spire of St Alkmund's Church disappeared when the inner ring road (St Alkmund's Way) was built in 1967-68, thus destroying one of the finest Georgian squares in England.

Herbert Spencer's birthplace ceased to exist

when a large area east of the River Derwent was cleared for the building of the same inner ring road, and the blacksmith's forge went at that time. The Old Mayor's Parlour was demolished in 1948 and provided a small car-park for Corporation buses and, latterly, has seen a huge excavation which has concerned Derbeians greatly.

Besides the changes recorded on *Old Derby Revisited* there have been many others in the city. Two fine halls, at Markeaton and Darley, have been demolished – a sad loss – but few can regret the disappearance of the Ice Factory in The Morledge. The replacement of the Midland Railway Station by its modern counterpart is viewed with mixed feelings.

These changes are recorded in the following pages, but unlike the photographs taken for the 'Old Derby' article, these were not taken to record changes but for purely personal interest. There are exceptions, however. A few were taken to illustrate a booklet called *Derby Markets and Bus Station* (1964) and others were taken especially for my book *Derby Old and New* where old scenes were contrasted with the same scene now. A third edition of that book has resulted in other photographs of changes.

The timbered Elizabethan house known as the Old Mayor's Parlour stood in Tenant Street until its demolition in 1948. Now it is the site of the infamous 'Derby Hole', where more than one plan for a hotel has been aborted.

Markeaton Hall was built by the Mundys in 1775. The hall and park were presented to the town by Mrs Mundy in 1928, but the hall was allowed to deteriorate until it was deemed necessary to demolish it in 1964. Here it is seen from the gardens, the orangery seen on the left still standing and providing refreshment for the many visitors to this fine park.

The marble Markeaton Hall fountain, surmounted by fine wrought-iron work, was brought from Italy by a member of the Mundy family. At the time of writing it stands in a garden in Matlock Bath.

The stables behind the Orangery were approached through a gateway beneath a Dovecote. This too was demolished with the hall, but the stables now house a small craft centre.

The house called Darley Abbey was built in 1737 by William Wesley, one-time Mayor of Derby. Darley Abbey park and house were purchased by Derby Corporation in 1931 and opened by His Royal Highness the Duke of Kent. After being occupied by Derby Central School, the hall was demolished in 1962. Today a small portion of the house seen on the left, is used as a tea room for visitors.

When the Council House was built in 1939-40 its prospect over the River Derwent was enhanced by
pleasant gardens which included an ornamental fishpond with two bronze figures of tortoises. With the
building of the new law courts nearby, the gardens have been reduced and the pool is no more, but the
tortoises have found a new resting place in a pool fronting the hall in Allestree Park.

Popularly known as the 'Boy and Goose', this statue stood close by the pool in the River Gardens, having been moved there from the Market Place when the Council House was built. Today it stands within the Assembly Rooms complex, close to its original position.

This view up stream from Exeter Bridge shows how industrialised the Derwent was some 40 years ago. The Power Station built in 1922 has gone together with the conglomeration of buildings to the right, but the historic Silk Mill remains, now the home of the Industrial Museum.

The River Derwent from St Mary's Bridge in 1940. This view of the Derwent taken from St Mary's Bridge shows the Silk Mill seemingly lost among the same buildings seen in the previous photograph. The Power Station was demolished in 1971 and the Sowter Mill, which fronts it, is no longer a dusty flour mill. The concrete span of Causey Bridge now cuts across the foreground.

Bridge Gate from St Mary's Bridge. St Mary's and St Alkmund's churches are seen here from St Mary's Bridge with its chapel in 1964. Bridge Gate and St Alkmund's Church disappeared with the building of the inner ring road in 1967-68.

The Great Northern Railway came to Derby in 1878, crossing the northern edge of the town on a viaduct to the station in Friar Gate. It closed in 1964 and this photograph of Ford Street was taken in the 1970s, prior to the demolition of the viaduct. For many years the arches were used by small businesses, as seen here. A story which was associated with the arches linked them with the popular song *Underneath the Arches* which was written by Chesney Allen, when Flanagan and Allen were appearing at the Derby Hippodrome in Green Lane, although Chesney Allen denied there was any connection.

Many interesting views could be seen from the top of the viaduct, and this one, photographed from where it ended abruptly at Willow Row, shows the route of the original railway continuing eastwards where it obliterated Cherry Street. An old warehouse is seen in the distance and today several new buildings have appeared, including that of Derbyshire Countryside Limited.

This close-up view of the warehouse now a business premises shows it well worthy of preservation.

In the first photograph of Ford Street, the bridge over Brook Street is seen. This view looks down on the backs of the houses.

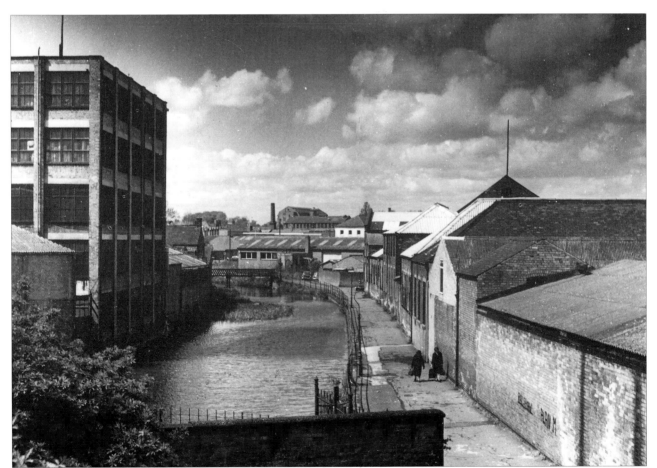

This view from the viaduct of Brook Walk, with its many factories, could not be repeated.

The viaduct as far as Friar Gate Bridge, waiting for the possible continuation of St Alkmund's Way. Where the arches joined Friar Gate Bridge, the first few were used as stables for the horses in the days of the horse-drawn trams. Here are seen the tramlines leading from Friar Gate into the stable area.

The remains of Friar Gate Bridge looking west to the site of the railway station platform.

The derelict Friar Gate Station looking east.

Situated just outside the town to the east, this viaduct carried the railway over the Little Eaton Canal near Breadsall village. It was demolished when Sir Frank Whittle Way was built.

The old Midland Railway Station – later Derby Station – was refaced in 1892, fronting on the original Thompson Station of 1840. The modern station (1985) is an incongruous centrepiece among a group of significant Victorian buildings. The clock pediment of the station hides insignificantly at the end of the railway car-park.

This simple wooden structure carried the tow-path of the Derby Canal across the Derwent near The Morledge. The canal was built in 1796. It was closed after the last war and the bridge, for some years very unsafe for pedestrians, was closed in 1959 and demolished shortly afterwards.

The road from the Morledge to the Cattle Market crossed Derby Canal on Cattle Market Bridge, and this view shows the derelict state of the canal in 1960. Today a few stones of the bridge parapet remain to identify the scene, now occupied by Cockpit Hill car-park.

Gandy's Cheese Warehouse at Cattle Market Bridge, dated 1820.

A short stretch of canal called Bridgewater Wharf branched off behind the warehouse. The area was cleared for the building of the inner ring road in the late 1970s.

Another area cleared for the inner ring road was the Cattle Market which stood just over the Cattle Market Bridge. This was moved to The Meadows in 1970.

This view of the Ice Factory shows some of the buildings near the River Derwent. The area was cleared in 1931 for the building of the Bus Station and Morledge Market a few years later.

The Ice Factory.

This grim Ice Factory building dominated the Morledge from the turn of the century when it was built by Sir Alfred Haslam, the pioneer of refrigeration on ships. The Pure Ice and Cold Storage Co Ltd advertised that, apart from making ice, it offered cold storage for meat, eggs, butter and cheese. Fur coats were also stored there. Its decline began with the introduction of the home freezer and later the building was used for other purposes. In 1975, tenders were invited for the demolition of the four-storey Victorian monstrosity and this took place before the end of the decade, just after these two photographs were taken.

The open Morledge Market in 1964 revives memories. To the right are the market offices.

When taking photographs for a booklet called *Derby Markets and Bus Station* in 1964, I took these two views from the top of the Ice Factory. The Morledge has seen several changes in the intervening years, the main one being the building of the Crown and County Courts on the site of the open Morledge Market. The houses on Cockpit Hill on the immediate left were demolished for the Eagle Centre where the 'open' market is now housed.

When this photograph was taken in 1977, this block of buildings in Tenant Street near its junction with Derwent Street was due for demolition. The 'DCOD' on the shop front indicates the Derby Corporation Omnibus Department restaurant – the wartime Civic Restaurant. Derby Corporation and Derbyshire County Council had offices on the corner, later occupied by Philipson's Seed Merchant. A glimpse of the new Assembly Rooms is seen across the Market Place.

This view of the Council House was taken from a window of the Old Mayor's Parlour just before it was demolished in 1948. It is an interesting record of the roofs of the old town.

When the Old Mayor's Parlour was demolished, the site was used as a bus park before being turned into a small open space with a subway leading to the Council House. In recent times the area, together with Tenant Street has been lost in the infamous 'Hole'.

The Market Hall was opened in 1866 and this view of the southern end shows the Fish and Poultry Market which was added in 1926. This addition was demolished in 1981 just after this photograph was taken, the stalls now being housed in Lock-up Yard, off the Cornmarket. In 1985 the area was named Osnabrück Square in connection with twinning of Derby with that German city.

The Eagle Centre, opened in 1975, occupied the site of Castlefields Lace Mill built by the Boden family in the early nineteenth century.

Built in 1805, the Methodist Church in King Street was another important building sacrificed to St Alkmund's Way when the inner ring road was built in 1967-68. It was replaced by a multi-storey car-park in 1971.

Since the article 'Old Derby' (mentioned in previous pages) was published in 1948, this view of Derby School in the churchyard of St Peter's has unfortunately been hidden from St Peter's Street by a modern addition to the church.

A greengrocer delivers outside Herbert Spencer's birthplace (see plaque) in Exeter Street just before the area was cleared to make way for the building of the inner ring road across the river.

Taken at about the same time as the previous quiet scene in Exeter Street, a busy St Peter's Street in the 1960s is a great contrast. The imposing Midland Drapery building was demolished in 1970 and the Odeon Cinema closed in 1965.

Also taken in the 1960s, this photograph shows East Street as seen from St Peter's Churchyard. The Boots' Chemist shop on the corner was built in 1890 and with its statues of Derby worthies is still one of the more attractive buildings in the city.

Looking down St Peter's Street in the 1970s. Today the underground toilets are surmounted by a clock tower and two columns of ornamental stonework.

To end on a frivolous note, one wonders if anyone has been fined twice for parking on both sides of Amen Alley at the same time!

On the Outskirts

During the past half-century, Derby, like all our towns and cities, has expanded. To the south the little hamlet of Sinfin is now lost in an urban complex which includes a church, houses, shops and a large supermarket. Nostalgia still takes me back to this haunt of my school days shown in the following photographs.

The hamlet of Sinfin. This wintry scene, taken over 50 years ago, shows a row of cottages which still stand. The road links Normanton with Barrow-on-Trent.

The lane ran from Sinfin to Barrow-on-Trent and this photograph taken about a mile beyond Sinfin was taken on the same day. The milk lorry was collecting from outlying farms, the one shown here was always known to us as Mather's Farm.

Today the farm has been replaced by a church and the lorry by a bus, only the tree and my memory identifying the scene.

At the junction of a lane from Twyford, the lorry collected the milk churns from Mather's Farm as well as from a horse and cart which came from a farm at Arleston on the Twyford road. Today this spot is lost in the centre of a heavily built-up area.

Another picture of the junction of a lane from Twyford.

Homeward Bound. Taken in better weather, this poignant scene was caught on the road to Barrow-on-Trent where no doubt the boys had had a happy but tiring day beside the canal.

The same scene today, only identified by my knowing the area intimately. (These two photographs appear in the author's book *Derbyshire Old and New*)

These riders had right of way in Stenson Road in 1946.

The bend on the left is Stenson Road seen in the previous picture.

The extension of the town beyond Allestree towards Quarndon meant the loss of pleasant hilly countryside. I lived in Allestree village for much of my early childhood and grew to know the area well, revisiting it in 1938 with my wife when the following photographs were taken. The changes today are remarkable.

Allestree Lane runs from Kedleston Road and, where it made a sharp right turn into Allestree village, Woodlands Road continued straight on through a gate to climb an open field to Quarndon. A simple device in the form of a hanging weight kept the gate closed.

Woodlands Road. The open road to Quarndon was a very popular spot for children in winter.

Post-war development made the road quite unsuitable for such activities.

Where the road crested the hill, a farming scene made a delightful picture. Today it is here joined by Westbank Avenue.

Beneath the beeches. Rows of splendid beech trees graced the hilltop and horse riders complete the scene. Today self-set silver birches have replaced the beeches.

Gathering beech nuts at Quarndon.

This small orchard at Hollies Farm in Allestree is well remembered from 70 years ago when I lived in nearby Robincroft. Photographed in 1950, it remained an unchanged oasis among extensive housing development until it too succumbed, the farm being converted into housing units in 1993.

This view across an open field in Markeaton Lane was taken before the crematorium was built there in 1956. Today the scene is transformed by attractive lawns and well-established shrubs.

The cottage seen in the distance on the right in the previous picture stood close to the junction of Markeaton Lane with Ashbourne Road. Today no trace of it remains.

These truncated remains of a tower windmill stood just off Station Road in Mickleover. Standing in open fields it became surrounded by a housing development and was eventually demolished and is now only commemorated in nearby street names.

In 1638, Sir Robert Wilmot of Chaddesden Hall had these six almshouses built facing the west door of the church. They were demolished in 1963, and this show of philanthropy, still evident in many of our villages, is now but a memory in Chaddesden.

Before the Reservoirs

During the past 60 years no less than six major new reservoirs have been built in the county. The largest of these, the Ladybower, was completed in the Upper Derwent Valley in 1945, and resulted in the destruction of the villages of Derwent and Ashopton. In 1967 the hamlet of Goyts Bridge in the Goyt Valley disappeared beneath the waters of the Errwood Reservoir. There was loss of farmland when the Ogston Reservoir flooded the Amber Valley and there was further loss when the Foremark and Staunton Harold Reservoirs were built in the south of the county. King George VI opened the Ladybower Reservoir and the newest reservoir, Carsington, was opened by the Queen Elizabeth II in 1992. The following photographs remind us what these valleys looked like before they disappeared beneath the waters.

Probably the greatest change in the county in the past 60 years was the building of the Ladybower Reservoir in the Upper Derwent Valley, thereby completely changing the face of the landscape. Work began in 1935 and this view of the early stages shows the conglomeration of huts etc., at the place where the dam wall was to be constructed between the villages of Ashopton and Bamford.

The untouched valley between Ashopton and Derwent villages.

The village of Ashopton was demolished about 1943 and the Sheffield to Manchester road which ran through it now crosses the valley on the viaduct. The village lay to the right of it.

When the reservoir began to fill work on the embankment was well advanced. Being built of earth but with a concrete core and stone facing on the water side, surplus water could not flow over the top and in the foreground is one of two overflows which take surplus water beneath the embankment.

Another view showing the filling valley.

These views of the village of Derwent were taken just before it was engulfed by the rising waters. The hall of 1672 was demolished and the seventeenth-century Packhorse Bridge taken down stone by stone and re-erected higher up the river.

Another view of the Packhorse Bridge taken from the grounds of the Hall. Bridge Farm is seen behind.

Close by and apparently peeping over the parapet of the wall of the Hall grounds is the stone figure of Peeping Tom. This may now be seen in the Information Centre at the Derwent Dam higher up the valley.

Derwent Church, built in 1876, was demolished except for the tower. Its font of 1662 from a previous church is now in Hope Church.

The church tower stood for a few years and in times of drought was entered by visitors, but was ultimately demolished as unsafe. The village war memorial was re-erected high on the hillside.

The severe drought of 1959 exposed the dried-up course of the river and the boundary wall of the Hall grounds.

Also exposed were the foundations of the Packhorse Bridge.

Today the Packhorse Bridge again spans the River Derwent higher up the valley at Slippery Stones on a former packhorse route.

When these photographs were taken over 40 years ago, Goyts Bridge in the Goyt Valley was one of the loveliest and quietest spots in the county, visited by ramblers and a few adventurous motorists. Here the River Goyt was crossed by stepping stones and a ford, while the small Moorstone Brook, seen joining it here, was crossed by a typical packhorse bridge. Some 300 years ago this spot was lively with packhorse trains, 30 or 40 packhorses laden with salt from Cheshire on their way east across Derbyshire or carrying grain or coal in the opposite direction.

Goyts Bridge. A few cars have found their way here to park beside the river. Today this delightful spot lies beneath the waters of the Errwood Reservoir built by the Stockport Corporation in 1967 who dismantled the packhorse bridge and re-erected it higher up the valley. The reservoir is now a very popular venue, motorists having to be regulated along the narrow roads from several car-parks.

The re-erected packhorse bridge now carries a footpath over the river higher up the valley.

Ogston Reservoir. The peace of the Amber Valley is seen here to the south of Ashover in 1950. This had been shattered when the Ashover Light Railway was built in 1925 but tranquillity returned when it closed 24 years later.

The route of the railway is on the raised embankment and bridge abutment where it crossed the River Amber near Ogston Hall. In 1958 the valley was flooded for the building of the Ogston Reservoir and these scenes have gone forever.

In 1957, the New Brook between Staunton Harold and Melbourne was flooded beneath a new reservoir. This view of the valley taken in 1950 shows Furnace Farm which took its name from an eighteenth-century charcoal-fired ironworks close by, which was excavated before this bit of industrial archaeology was lost beneath the waters.

Milk being collected from the top of the drive at Furnace Farm before the days when large tankers took over from milk churns.

Upstream from Furnace Farm, Calke Mill was wedged in the narrowing valley. The disused corn mill, thought to date from the sixteenth century, stood beyond the haystack.

In this view the farmhouse is seen across the farmyard with the mill on the immediate right.

As in so many of these old mills, the weight of the millstones has caused the collapse of the timber supports and here they lie in disorder.

Forgotten Bridge at Calke. This impressive stone bridge spans the brook near the mill. It was built by Sir Henry Harpur Crewe of Calke Abbey nearby to avoid passing through Ticknall and Melbourne on his visits to London. Legend has it that passing over it when nearly completed, he told the workmen that when he returned he would keep his eyes open to see that it was finished. He was killed while horse riding in London and, 'tis said, his eyes could not be closed until he had passed over the bridge.' Today the remains of the bridge, the farm and the mill, lie beneath the waters of Staunton Harold reservoir.

The valley of Scow Brook near Carsington was chosen as the site of Derbyshire's newest reservoir. A single road crossed the valley, and beside it stood a lonely chapel seen in the middle distance.

The chapel's isolated position stems from the troubled times of the 17th century when the Established Church forced dissenters to worship at a specified distance from villages. The chapel was on the upper floor, the room below was a stable.

The chapel has been restored and enlarged, to serve as the headquarters of the Rangers who are responsible for the maintenance of the reservoir site amenities. The reservoir was opened in 1992 by Her Majesty, Queen Elizabeth II.

Derbyshire's Mills

The Derbyshire rivers were dammed in the eighteenth century to provide the power for the cotton mills built on their banks and also for the small corn mills located in the delightful dales. Many of the cotton mills have been put to other uses, but unfortunately too many of the small mills which graced the dales have either disappeared or been converted to residences, while the few windmills, except at Heage and Dale Abbey, are in a ruinous state. Like the cornmills, those at Belper and Findern have been converted into pleasant dwellings.

Taken in 1960, this photograph shows the mill complex started by the Strutts beside the River Derwent at Belper. North Mill, the five-storied building fronting the tall chimney, was built in 1797 to be followed early in the next century by the West Mill, seen on the right. The tall chimney was taken down stone by stone in recent years because it was unsafe in high winds, while the dominant East Mill close by is no longer a cotton mill.

A closer view of the Victorian clock tower of West Mill, seen from Bridge Street. The ornate clock tower was added in 1897 to mark the Jubilee of Queen Victoria, and this Belper landmark, together with the mill, was demolished in 1962.

The very unusual Round Mill – actually octagonal – was built in 1813 and stood close by West Mill. It is seen here in process of its demolition in 1959. East Mill of 1912 is seen in the background.

The Strutts' influence extended down the Derwent to Milford where Jedediah Strutt built another cotton mill complex about 1780. He was also responsible for the bridge over the river being built. This view from it was taken in 1945.

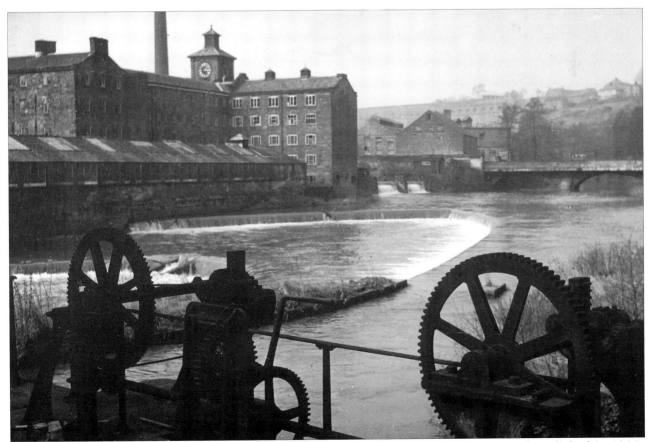

Another view of the Milford Mill seen from across the weir. The mill buildings were demolished in 1964 and have been replaced by modern buildings.

Chain Bridge at Milford. This suspension bridge built in 1826 spanned the river just below the weir in the previous photograph. It was dismantled just after these photographs were taken in 1945.

During the past 60 years a number of old water mills have disappeared from our valleys. This cornmill, known as Carter's Mill, was a feature in Lathkill Dale. These three photographs record its dilapidation over 50 years ago.

This view of the interior of Carter's Mill shows how the floor had collapsed under the weight of the millstones.

Left: Taken many years after the previous photographs, this shows a further deterioration of the mill. The water wheel was removed during World War Two and today nothing remains of the building, although a millstone may be discovered on the overgrown site. Only the millpool indicates that here once stood Carter's Mill. Right: Two mills, one at each end, identify Mill Dale, but the corn mill seen here in 1957 in the little hamlet of Milldale has been demolished. A reminder that a mill once stood here is a millstone lying in the River Dove and used by villages when collecting water from the river. Lode Mill upstream still stands.

Repton Brook, which runs from near Hartshorne to Repton, once powered no less than seven mills. This thatched example is situated to the south of Repton and was demolished soon after this view was taken.

Melbourne Corn Mill situated below the mill dam built by George Sorocold. The building is now a house.

'James and Sarah'. When I took these photographs of the twin tower windmills at Riddings near Alfreton in 1950, I was fortunate in meeting a gentleman who asked, "Would you like to see over them?" The mills were no longer in use and we climbed 90 feet into the cap of one to see how it turned into the wind by a gear wheel running on a circular cast-iron rack. He told me the mills were built in 1877 by the local coalmine owner, James Oakes, who named them after himself and his wife Sarah, although the windmill 'Sarah' never worked, being built too close to 'James'. In calm weather the millstones were turned by steam and later a diesel engine which continued in use after the mills lost their sails in 1948. No doubt the pigeons housed in the tall dovecote waxed fat on spilled corn! The gentleman showed me what little was left of the machinery and when I left he insisted on giving me a wrought-iron candle-stick used in a shallow coalmine close by as he was so pleased to meet 'someone so interested in these old mills'. Today a modern factory stands on the site.

Left: A view inside the 'James' mill showing the chute which fed the grain into the hopper and on to the enclosed millstones. The gear wheel was turned by the sails and meshed with a smaller one. This in turn rotated the shaft seen behind the chain. thus turning the stones within the wooden casing, and right (top): A close-up of the gears shows that the teeth of the smaller wheel which were made of wood – apple, I believe. These were inserted through holes in the rim of the cast-iron wheel and held firm with wedges. They could be replaced easily when worn. Above right (bottom): The candlestick from the mills is shown here together with a lamp found in the debris of a demolished kiln. The lamp ran on crude oil which soaked up the wick projecting from the copper spout and the small reservoir at its base held a more flammable fuel which was lit to prime the heavy fuel.

South Normanton Windmill. While the towers of tower windmills still stand in the county there is only one post mill. Being made of wood this is not surprising and when I found this fine example at South Normanton in 1945 I took the opportunity to record it. The two figures give a good idea of its size. Taken down and stored, its promised re-erection has never materialised.

Millstones of South Normanton Windmill. The interior of the mill had collapsed and the millstones lay on the ground.

The windmill at Heage was in a ruinous state when this photograph was taken in 1960, the six sails almost gone. When it was built is not known, but it is recorded that it has graced this hilltop since 1850. In 1967 it was taken over by the Derbyshire County Council and restored to working order.

The Canals

The past half-century has seen a change on the canals from commercial traffic to pleasure craft. The Trent and Mersey Canal which follows the Trent Valley was the busiest in the county and the following photographs will bring back memories of the commercial activity. These photographs have been used as illustrations in several books, and make one wonder if perhaps canal traffic will return one day?

The Trent and Mersey Canal was a great source of interest to me in my younger days and the gaily-painted boats were to become a fruitful source of subjects for my camera in later years. Many of the boats were owned by Fellows, Morton and Clayton and this one is seen near Barrow-on-Trent in the late 1940s.

Ice-bound at Stenson. Not all days were as idyllic as that shown in the previous photograph and this scene shows boats being freed from ice on a winter's morning at Stenson Lock.

The Clock Warehouse at Shardlow. After the opening of the canal throughout in 1777, Shardlow developed into an inland port and its importance is shown by this fine warehouse built in 1780. When this photograph was taken in 1948 it was used for milling animal feedstuffs but today it is a restaurant.

Originally built as a warehouse in 1792, Shardlow Mill was also used for milling feedstuffs. Like the Clock Warehouse, boats and barges could unload under the arches. Today it has been converted into desirable flats, being modified after fires.

Millstones from the Shardlow Mill in 1948. The one on the left is made of segments held together with an iron band. These burr-stones were imported from France.

Canal traffic began to decline in the 1960s, although boats continued to pass through Shardlow. Here, two tied up, are a reminder of busier days. Some of these narrow boats have been converted into pleasure boats and together with numerous small craft make the canal perhaps busier than it ever was even in its heyday.

This shows the Cromford and High Peak Railway which connected with the Peak Forest Canal at Whaley Bridge. The Sheep Pastures Incline, seen here, was one of nine rope-worked inclines which were incorporated when the line was built in 1831. Today the lines have been removed and the route is now the High Peak Trail with the engine shed providing a view of times past.

This tramway was built by George Stephenson to carry limestone from his quarries at Crich to the lime kilns which he built at Ambergate in 1840-41. The latest kilns were demolished in 1957 and this photograph of the incline was taken just before the track was removed to the Talyllyn Railway in North Wales.

When William Jessop built the Cromford Canal in 1793, he carried it across the Amber Valley at Bull Bridge on an aqueduct over a lane, the river and main road. Traffic lights were installed when the main road beneath the canal proved too narrow for modern traffic as seen here just before it was demolished in 1968. In 1839-40 George Stephenson carried his Derby to York railway line beneath the canal as seen on the left. This bridge also has been demolished.

Bull Bridge Aqueduct. In this view of the canal above the road, the parapet of the railway is seen just beyond the figure at the stop lock the boat being directly over the road.

View from Aqueduct. Traffic on the road and railway is seen from the same spot as the previous photograph.

Site of the Bull Bridge Aqueduct. Travellers along the A610 road at Bull Bridge today see no evidence of the canal and the railway which crossed here.

Bull Bridge Lime Kilns. The remains of five lime kilns stand beside the aqueduct, seen here from the lane called Drovers' Way which passed beneath the aqueduct. The lime came from Hilt's Quarry at Crich and the kilns ran from 1780 until the 1930s. This photograph was taken in the 1960s and even less remains of these industrial 'castles' today.

Down on the Farm

The increasing pace of life has had its effect on farming and the following photographs show the more gentle pace of life. Here my nostalgia was strongest as I sorted out the old photographs for this section, for mechanisation has completely changed the country scene. Haymaking is no longer a manual activity, and for children the ride on the haycart is a pleasure of the past, as too are the games of hide and seek in the stackyard. Haystacks having been replaced by ugly piles of big black plastic bags. The corn had to be stooked to be carted from the fields to the farm to await the visit of the thresher. One morning we would be up early to search the hillside for the tell-tale puff of smoke which heralded the approach of the traction engine pulling the threshing machine. The following days in the stackyard were full of excitement, of noise, dust and scurrying rats, with the frightening slap of the huge belt which ran from the reaction engine to the threshing machine. Today the corn is cut and threshed in the fields by the combine harvester and the grain is carried to the store.

In more recent years the changes on the farm have been remarkable. Farms have become larger units and many farms situated in the village have been converted into housing units, stables and cowsheds into desirable flats grouped round a courtyard, once the farmyard. Isolated farms in the Peak District continue farming but also cater for visitors and caravanners. The apparently

lazy days of the horse and cart have given way to the tractor in the lanes and fields, while the pony and trap has been overtaken by the Land Rover and Volvo.

'Sons of the Soil'.

Chain harrowing on the hills above Dovedale.

Chain harrowing at Quarndon near Derby.

A winter's day at Stenson in South Derbyshire.

Orphans at Glutton Grange near
Earl Sterndale in the Upper Dove
Valley.

Meeting dad home from the farm at Glutton Bridge in the Upper Dove Valley.

Sunday morning at Swarkestone.

A quiet day at
Ashover Hay
near Ashover.

On the hills above the Via Gellia.

Scene in Tamworth Street, Duffield.

On the Ashbourne Road
near Kirk Langley.

In Markeaton village near Derby.

The Travellers' Rest stands close to Axe Edge between Buxton and Leek.

Two horse-power in Breadsall village near Derby.

Carting roots from the fields at Swarkestone.

Carting manure to the fields at Stenson.

Ploughing a lone furrow at Alfreton.

Out to the fields at Smisby Manor in south Derbyshire.

Homeward bound at Holbrook.

Unharnessing at Gratton Grange near Elton.

A quiet day at Radbourne.

In the Via Gellia near Bonsall.

Returning from the fields at Barrow-on-Trent.

This scene in Bakewell is unlikely to be repeated today.

Awaiting the next harvest.

Away to the field, at Swarkestone.

Rest day on a farm at Kedleston.

Time for a chat near Kedleston.

Ancient and modern
near Willington.

Milking time at Chellaston, again a scene unlikely to be seen today.

Approaching Matlock on a very quiet A6 road.

A potential traffic-stopping scene on Swarkestone Bridge.

Scything an awkward corner at Earl Sterndale.

Milking in the fields at Parwich.

The pony and trap can still be
seen in Repton today, but it was
a common sight years ago.

A quiet scene in Thorpe near Dovedale.

Turning the hay near Flash on the Staffordshire border.

Cutting the corn before the advent of the combine harvester. Beside the A6 road near Belper.

Haymaking in the Upper Dove Valley with Parkhouse Hill in the background.

Mowing near Dove Head on Axe Edge.

Turning the hay by hand in the fields above Wirksworth.

In the fields near Hathersage.

Turning the hay above Bradwell near Castleton.

Out to the fields at Kniveton.

Day's work done at Kniveton.

A busy scene at Findern where the dutch barns are almost full.

The last load and a ride home.

A wintry scene at Ingleby.

Conversation Piece.

Loading lime at Elvaston near Derby.

A word in passing. A scene on the hills above Duffield.

Setting potatoes near Blackbrook.

In the village of Barrow-on-Trent.

Preparing the fields.

A well-stocked stackyard at Twyford beside the River Trent in the late 1940s. Note the cart beside the stable and the geese which held undisputed sway on the farm. Stackyards and farm buildings are ideal for hide and seek and I well remember being chased by these ferocious birds who objected to our invasion of their domain!

This view taken in 1990 from the same spot as the previous photograph clearly shows how mechanisation has completely taken over on the farm.

In more recent years a remarkable change has taken place on the farm, for many farmhouses and buildings have been converted into housing units. James Oakes built this model farm at Riddings but it was no longer in use when this photograph was taken in 1983. The unusual octagonal seed store, now a listed building, is the centre piece in a cobbled courtyard surrounded by mews dwellings.

This farm at Ambergate, seen here at milking time many years ago, is now the social and sports club of a local firm.

Milk delivery at Duffield.

Milking time at Eyam.

Some More Changes

A quiet day on Cavendish Bridge at Shardlow in 1945. The bridge was built in 1758-59 to replace Wilden Ferry and took its name from the Duke of Devonshire who had contributed most of its cost.

The bridge was swept away by the floodwaters of the angry River Trent in 1947 and the Derby-Leicester-London road was cut.

A single track Bailey Bridge was quickly erected on the butments and this served with traffic lights for ten years until a new concrete span was built a short distance down river.

Cavendish Bridge Tollhouse. The tollhouse stood on the Derbyshire bank. This was demolished but the Swithland slate tablet giving the toll charges which was on the pediment above the doorway was preserved and now stands close by.

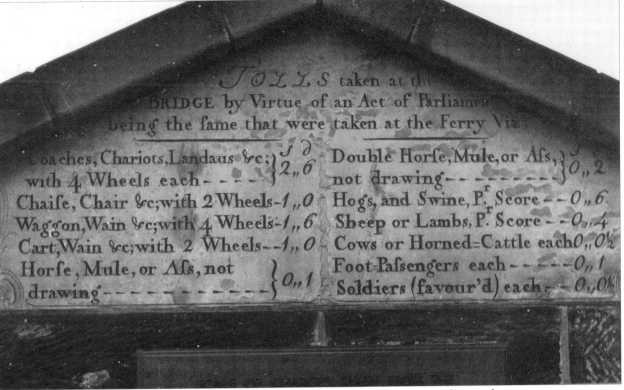

As can be seen here, the toll charges make fascinating reading today.

Known locally as Ha'penny Bridge, this bridge built in 1792 over the River Derwent at Ambergate took its name from the toll paid by pedestrians. Like Cavendish Bridge this too replaced a ferry and the tollhouse seen here was called Ferry House. This was demolished in 1964 and the only record of this being a toll bridge is perpetuated in its name.

This scene beside the main road at Cromford photographed in 1940 shows Glenorchy Chapel and Manse built by Sir Richard Arkwright in 1777. The chapel took its name from Lady Glenorchy who bought it in 1785. She was a lady who used her great wealth in encouraging religious revival wherever she went. In 1851 Sir George Newnes, the famous publisher, was born in the Manse, his father being the congregational minister at that time. The chapel and manse were sacrificed in the name of road widening, revealing Arkwright's later mill, no longer in cotton production.

The very narrow Scarthin Nick at Cromford was cut by Robert, son of Sir Richard, who built Glenorchy Chapel nearby.

The original narrow Scarthin Nick, cut in 1815, became a bottle neck when increasing traffic on the A6 road called for its widening, seen here in progress in 1963.

A view taken from a steam train speeding over the viaduct in Monsal Dale may revive the memories of travellers on one of the most scenic stretches of line in the country. Opened in 1863, the line was 'chopped' by the 'Beeching Axe' in 1968 and today is part of the Monsal Trail.

A train passes through a cutting above Millers Dale in 1963.

The same view in 1990 showing the Monsal Trail and how quickly nature has taken over

The road below Mam Tor was constructed in the early nineteenth century to avoid the steep Winnats Pass. It was built over the residue of shale which through the centuries has slipped down the slopes of Mam Tor and, being unable to cope with the weight of modern traffic, continued to slip requiring frequent repairs.

A slip which occurred in 1977 resulted in the road being abandoned.

Left: Today the name 'Cook' is synonymous with travel all over the world. The tablet over the doorway of this humble cottage in Quick Close, Melbourne, indicates the birthplace, in 1808, of Thomas Cook. The name of Quick Close came from the quick or hawthorn which Melbourne grew to hedge the 'new' railways which Cook used in his travel excursions. The cottage has been demolished, but nearby is a group of almshouses and chapel which were donated to the town. Right: An interesting feature in Kings Newton which has disappeared is an arch of whale bones. The name has been perpetuated in Jawbone Lane and today two tall bones front a new bungalow lower down the lane.

This ancient crossing of the River Trent at Twyford fell into disuse following the building of the bridge at Willington in 1839, but the ferry continued to be used by the farmer nearby, until after the last war as he owned fields on the opposite side of the river. Here he milked his cows and in this photograph taken in 1950, is seen carrying the milk churn from the ferry back to the farm. The boat was pulled across the river by means of the chain.

The name Monkey Bridge came from the tale of an itinerant entertainer who toured the country with a monkey. It performed on a rope hanging from the bridge, but unfortunately the performance and the monkey came to a sad end when the rope broke. Today the cliff face and the bridge have been completely quarried away and are but a memory.

Monkey Bridge stood on an old road which ran from Middleton by Wirksworth along the edge of a limestone cliff into Wirksworth. When a quarry was cut behind the cliff, access to it was made by cutting through the cliff face and this bridge being built to carry the road.

When the Midland Railway was extended from Ambergate to Rowsley in 1849, it was intended to continue the line through Chatsworth Park. A 'quality' station, designed by Joseph Paxton, was built at Rowsley for the Duke of Devonshire who subscribed £50,000 to the scheme. A dispute between the Duke and the Duke of Rutland who wanted the line to go through Bakewell went to the House of Lords, which came down on the side of the Bakewell route. Paxton's Station, which does not stand on this route, has since been put to various uses.

In 1863 the railway was continued along the Wye Valley through Bakewell to Buxton and a second station – Rowsley Station – was built a short distance from the first. When the 'Beeching Axe' fell in 1967-68, the line was closed and the station taken down with the intention of re-erecting it at Peak Rail's premises at Buxton. Peak Rail hope one day to re-open this fine scenic route. These two photographs, taken when the station was being demolished, show its classical features. The area is now a small industrial estate and the marshalling yards are overgrown. Note the fine detail on the building.

This was the view of Great Rocks Dale seen by visitors stopping at the lay-by on the A6 at Topley Pike in the 1960s. It shows the less attractive face of the Peak District. Today, the lime kilns have gone and the quarry is gradually being filled with waste from the quarries higher up the dale. Nature is slowly recovering from this blot on the landscape.

Great Rocks Dale – the limeworks.

Visitors to the gallery, café and other attractions built around the old bottle kiln beside the A609 road at West Hallam may be surprised at this view taken before restoration. It is said that the pots, etc., for the hollow floors of the Milford Mill were made here. Two kilns were built in 1922 and operated with varied success before closing in the 1930s, then standing derelict for 50 years. One kiln had been demolished when in 1983 a local artist saw the potential of the remaining kiln and surrounding buildings and created the present delightful complex.

When this photograph was taken in 1948, the Petrifying Well at Matlock Bath could hardly be missed. The Matlocks had their heyday in Victorian and Edwardian times and the petrifying well was a great attraction. Here calcium-impregnated water dripped slowly on to simple objects such as bottles, boots and even bird's nests coating them with lime and thus 'petrifying' them. Soon after this photograph was taken the building was demolished to be replaced with a circular building of limestone which still stands, although this attraction is no longer fashionable.

The wooden headstock of Jinglers Head Mine, seen here at Wakebridge near Crich, was taken down by the Peak District Mines Historical Society for re-erection elsewhere.

Floods in the Trent Valley were a common sight many years ago. The historic Swarkestone Bridge is seen here from the south, snaking across the flooded meadows for nearly a mile to the actual river crossing at Swarkestone. The annual flooding became a thing of the past after the river was dredged some years ago, and the fields on the left were excavated for sand and gravel. the large workings are permanently flooded and provide a pleasant amenity for sailing.

Known locally as Forty Trunks, this magnificent cedar tree stands at the entrance to what was Potlock Farm near Willington. It is protected as being of 'special interest' but nevertheless is threatened by possible gravel extraction.

Train approaching Ambergate from the north on the line built between the present A6 and the Cromford Canal.

County Curiosities

In the 1920s, my schooldays were punctuated by red letter days when I visited my grandfather's farm at Hulland Ward Intakes, near Hulland Ward. He showed me the red swampy patch in the field from which the farm had taken its name of Red Mire Gap, and explained how the name 'intakes' came from the days when the Enclosure Acts dictated that field boundaries should be set back from road to prevent ambush by footpads and highwaymen. When the roads became free of these unwelcome characters these narrow strips were fenced or 'taken in' and the name 'intakes' was born. My grandfather also told me the story of Halter Devil Chapel which stood near the farm, of the farmer who tried to halter the Devil. Highwaymen and the Devil! My countryside of flowers and birds' nests was to become full of exciting people and fascinating features.

Landscape has always been my first love but scenery is always enhanced by its history and through the years I have photographed churches, houses, villages and curiosities like the Halter Devil Chapel. With many of the latter in my files I contributed articles on dovecotes, icehouses, village lock-ups, etc to the national magazines, and in 1952 approached the, now defunct, *Derbyshire Advertiser* – who always had time to feature the county's past – with the idea of a series to be called 'County Curiosities'. They agreed to a trial period of three months and, as after that time I heard nothing further from them, I continued sending four curiosities each month for nearly five years!

There was a large feedback from readers with suggestions that they should be published in book form and I put together a 'dummy' book, printing the photographs and writing out the captions to fit each page layout. Several publishers turned it down because, they said the cost of 164 photographs and the limited circulation made it not viable. For 20 years it was put on one side until, in 1979, when small pocket-size books were becoming popular, it was snapped up by a publisher, brought up to date, and appeared as *Curiosities of the Peak and South Derbyshire*. It ran to three reprints and when discontinued, I offered it to the *Derbyshire Countryside*. Revised again and slightly enlarged it is still selling as *Curiosities of Derbyshire and the Peak District*. The following pages show the variety of unusual features found in the county, the first two having appeared in the book.

Halter Devil Chapel. How this tiny chapel at Hulland Ward Intakes, near Mugginton, acquired the curious name of Halter Devil Chapel is one of the strangest tales ever told, yet it seems substantially true. One dark and stormy night in 1723, a farmer Francis Brown, decided to ride to Derby. He was very drunk and met his wife's protests with the remark "Ride I will, if I have to halter the Devil'. Finding what he thought was his horse in the paddock he was trying to put the halter over its head when a flash of lightning revealed the animal had horns. Brown was knocked senseless and on recovering was so convinced that it was the Devil he became a man of great sobriety and built this chapel adjoining his house. A stone tablet set on the house wall was lost when the present house was built in 1873 but it carried the inscription: 'Francis Brown in his old age; Did build him here a hermitage; Who being old and full of evil; Once on a time haltered the Devil.' The chapel measures only 14ft by 13ft and occasional services are held. It was never consecrated, being known simply by its strange soubriquet, but its founding and Francis Brown's death in 1731 are recorded in Mugginton Church.

Robin Hood's Picking Rods. These two round pillars set in a block of stone on Ludworth Moor, close to the Cheshire border, are shown on the Ordnance Survey map as 'Robin Hood's Picking Rods'. Theories that they were boundary stones or wayside crosses are discounted as they are socketed into the base, indicating that there were always two. Perhaps a more feasible explanation is the suggestion that they were used for stringing bows, and certainly the device would make the task much easier. This curiosity is situated about three miles south-west of Glossop beside a footpath crossing Cown Edge from Monks' Road to a minor road which drops into Chisworth. Basingwerk Abbey in Flintshire once owned land here and what is thought to be the base of a cross called Abbot's Chair lies beside Monks' Road. Perhaps the Picking Rods have some connection with the monks occupation of the area?

Many and varied are the tombstones found in our churchyards, ranging from the simple upright or flat tablets to the more elaborate showing the craft of the person buried. This example at Baslow is a solid block of stone which has been carved to represent a coffin with carvings in relief on the top, and a lifting ring at each end. Such a precaution may have been used in Scotland to discourage body snatchers!

Bob, Bold, Mona and Nell. Standing some 7ft high, this impressive memorial is situated in the garden of a cottage at Burbage, near Buxton. It was erected by a farmer who lived there many years ago to commemorate his four dogs – Bob, Bold, Mona and Nell – their names being carved on the sides.

A 'Walt Disney House'. This lonely building on the hillside below Curbar Edge overlooking the Derwent Valley is today embraced in the garden of a new house. The stepped conical roof of stone slabs has been cleverly set on the four walls and there are two floors and a fireplace.
Although it once housed a family, it has been suggested that it was a temporary jail for prisoners being taken across the Derbyshire hills.

Left: The cheese press was a fairly common feature in Derbyshire farms. This almost complete example stands outside a cottage at Kelstedge in the Amber Valley. Above: Combined Trough and Mounting Block. Many stone water troughs are to be seen in our farms and villages. In this example at the Miners' Arms at Milltown in the Amber Valley, the trough is combined with a mounting block more usually associated with inns, and is perhaps the only example of this dual purpose in the county.

This garden fence is made from the staves of old barrels. The shape and curve of each stave makes for a very attractive result and being oak and having been pickled probably in beer for many years it should be very durable. It makes a change from beer barrels converted into tubs. The fence is situated at Fiddler's Folly near Brailsford.

From Stable to Hospital. The Crescent and the Devonshire Royal Hospital, designed by John Carr of York, have graced Buxton since 1790. This building which houses the hospital was originally built as stables to serve the Crescent. The arrival of the railway reduced the use of the stables and in 1859 a part, and then in 1878 the entire building, was passed over by the 7th Duke of Devonshire to the Buxton Bath Charity. What was then the largest unsupported dome was erected over the open internal courtyard in 1881.

A Sundial for Horse Riders. This pedestal in the churchyard at Thorpe is topped by a sundial, but is too high to be used by a pedestrian. It may have been designed for horse riders, and as it stands among the graves, it is clearly not on its original site. This is supported by the fact that the gnomon is at an angle of 35 degrees exactly, whereas Thorpe stands on latitude 35 degrees three seconds. These three angle seconds make a difference in its location, and it is unlikely that Whitehurst, who made it, would make such a mistake.

Above: These toll road gateposts stand beside the Bamford road near the Marquis of Granby. A plaque nearby records that they stood originally on the Sheffield to Manchester road which was turnpiked in 1724. The posts with a new bar were re-erected by the Peak National Park in 1985.
Right: Anthony Bradshaw's Monument. This monument in Duffield Church was set up in 1600 by Anthony Bradshaw to commemorate his wife and 20 children. He lived to father three more. Perhaps even more remarkable is the rhyming acrostic on Anthony's name in the inscription to his family.

The Fountain at Youlgreave. Conduit Head is the official name of this reservoir at Youlgreave. It also has the more fanciful name of The Fountain and as can be seen it has stood in the main street since 1829.

Standing beside the main road through Barlborough this unusual gateway, with its bright colours and Greek words is curiously foreign to Derbyshire. It was built by the Rhodes family who once lived at Barlborough Hall in memory of a lady of the house, Felicity de Rodes. It is the entrance to a small garden of remembrance to the fallen of two world wars.

Left: Lying beside a road junction in the parish of Dethick, Lea and Holloway, this stone has always been known as the Gibbet Stone. It is thought that it was the socket for the post of a gibbet but there is no record of this. It has the appearance of a millstone, and in fact a cornmill stood beside the Lea Brook nearby. Right: The narrow 'V' stile which is common in Derbyshire sometimes has a circular clearance at the bottom for the foot. This example at Bamford has a much larger clearance and as this stile is the entrance to a small enclosure housing a trough and spring it could accommodate a bucket. This could be the only such example in the county.

'Fair Flora'. Curiosity is aroused at the sight of this statue in Stoke Wood near Grindleford. Erected over 150 years ago, the origin of Fair Flora is a mystery and it has been the subject of various legends. One explanation is that it came from Chatsworth Park and was given to the then owner of Stoke Hall nearby. But why 'Flora'. the Roman goddess of flowers. should now stand in this lonely wood is a mystery.

Left: It is not unusual for builders to include initials and the date, often in the form of coloured bricks, in their work. An interesting variation of this can be seen in a farm building at Longford Hall where the letters and figures have been formed by missing bricks giving ventilation which present a lacework effect. Above: The small brick church at Trusley was built in 1713 by William Coke who lived at the nearby hall. There are memorials to members of the family in the church, and the doorway and lead drainpipes are embossed with their coat of arms. It is believed they came from the old hall when it was demolished.

Gritstone troughs are found in various shapes and size. The farm buildings at Over Haddon which have been converted into a craft centre have this circle formed by segments of separate troughs.

My Derbyshire

In dividing this book into various sections, there were many photographs that were simply 'pictorial' and fitted into no particular category. A selection is shown here under the above title and I hope they give some idea of the beauty of Derbyshire as seen through my eyes with the aid of a camera. After 60 years, many of these scenes are still recognisable today and show the unchanging charm of the Derbyshire hills and dales. The pictures are arranged in no particular order, simply presented for the reader to enjoy.

Castle Rock towers above the River Wye in Cheedale.

The Cat and Fiddle is a welcome
sight seen across the moors west
of Buxton.

Geese once had
'right of way' in
Miller's Dale.

The famous High Tor and the River Derwent in Matlock Bath.

The end of the rainbow on Axe Edge, south of Buxton.

'The Downfall' where the River Kinder falls from the edge of Kinder Scout and feeds the Kinder Reservoir.

A dramatic view of Mam Tor at the head of Hope Dale.

This mountain road drops into the Via Gellia from Middleton-by-Wirksworth.

Water cum Jolly between Litton and Cressbrook Mills.

Above, left: A hardy silver birch graces the hillside with High Tor seen in the distance in Matlock Bath.

Above, right: Walkers approach Rushup Edge from Mam Tor.

The impressive Black Rocks near Cromford tower high above the village.

The Hope Valley with the shaly slopes of Mam Tor in the foreground.

One man and his dog beside the River Dove in Mill Dale.

The River Wye
flows sedately
beneath the
Sheepwash
Bridge in
Ashford-in-the-
Water.

A keen fisherman in the River Derwent at Cromford Bridge.

Chrome Hill in the Upper Dove Valley near Earl Sterndale.

Arbor Low, Derbyshire's prehistoric stone circle, is often referred to as the 'Stonehenge of the Midlands'.

The Stand at Crich, war memorial to the fallen of two world wars.

Milking time at Mugginton.

The River Wye at
Bakewell.

A quiet corner in Beeley village.

The churchyard slopes down to the River Derwent at Baslow.

Attractive cottages face Bar Brook at Nether End, Baslow.

Bar Brook at Nether End, Baslow.

Nelson's Monument stands on Birchin Edge above Baslow.

The fine Elizabethan hall at Somersal Herbert.

An unusual view of Bonsall village with its circular steps surmounted by a ruined cross.

The inn called the Cock and Pynot at Whittington, near Chesterfield, where the successful plot to overthrow James II was hatched in 1688. It is now a museum and called Revolution House.

An unusual view of the famous twisted spire of the church at Chesterfield.

The impressive dam wall at Derwent Reservoir in the Upper Derwent Valley.

The fourteenth-century church at Tideswell is popularly known as 'the Cathedral of the Peak'.

The statue of Sir Henry Royce in the Riverside Gardens in Derby. It now stands outside the Rolls-Royce site in Moor Lane.

A crumbling weir in Lathkill Dale.

The day's last task at Holme Farm, Kedleston.

'The Mourners' in Eyam
Churchyard. Their heads have now
gone.

Climbers at Cratcliff Tor, near
Birchover.

The railway viaduct in Monsal Dale
which aroused the wrath of John
Ruskin when it was built in 1861.

Hartington Hall of 1611 has long been a popular youth hostel.

High summer
at Hartington.

The infant Dane near the
Three Shires Head.

Thatched cottages in Osmaston. The one on the right was destroyed by fire some years ago.

View of the Amber Valley from Cocking Tor above Ashover.

A weir on the
River Kinder
in Hayfield.

An evening stroll at Fenny Bentley.

An ancient clapper
bridge in Bradford
Dale.

Dovedale seen from The Nabs. Not as dangerous as it looks.

Time for a chat in Tissington.

Walkers at the Ladybower Reservoir.

The Derwent Valley seen from Froggatt Edge.

The famous Crescent at Buxton was designed by John Carr for the Duke of Devonshire and has stood here since 1784.

Cork Stone on Stanton Moor.

Evening at Abney.

A quiet day at Alport in Bradford Dale.

Frost reveals leaks in Wigwell Aquaduct which carries the Cromford Canal over the River Derwent at Lea Bridge.

A country lane near Crich.

Mill weir in the Via Gellia near Bonsall.

Old cottages in
Tideswell.

A hardy fisherman
beside the River
Derwent at Duffield
Bridge.

The main street of Ashford-in-the-Water seen from the old pump house. Today, new houses fill the space on the right.

The mill pool near Cressbrook Mill in Water cum Jolly in the Wye Valley.

A gentle stroll in the valley of Repton Brook, south of Repton.

Repton School seen through the Norman archway. The film *Goodbye Mr Chips* was shot on location here.

Repton schoolboys skating on the flooded meadows near Willington.

The lowing herd at Barrow-on-Trent.

A peaceful scene beside the river at Barrow-on-Trent.

Flooded meadows at Barrow-on-Trent.

A very cold winter when the river
froze at Barrow-on-Trent.

Frost follows the floods at
Twyford.

A winter's day at Ingleby.

Kings Newton under snow.

Muffins for tea? A
misty day at
Kings Newton.

Young riders beside The Green at Bretby.

A pleasant scene beside
Ashbourne Church.

Swans glide across the mill pool at
Longford.

Norbury Manor House and Church.

Scene across the mere at Monyash.

Walk Through Bradford Dale in 1994

This book began with a description of a walk taken in 1939 and ends with another walk in 1994. The itinerary is very similar – a visit to a lovely dale, another attractive village and a call at its church. In both cases there is little change in the scenery in the intervening 55 years, but the creation of the Peak National Park and the great increase in car ownership has created problems with the enormous number of visitors to the county. The hamlet of Alport stands at the confluence of the Rivers Lathkill and Bradford and it is from there that this walk continues up Bradford Dale and returns through the village of Youlgreave.

These two photographs show the River Lathkill, seen here from the bridge in Alport, held in check by small weirs, and then tumbles rapidly the last few yards to join the Bradford.

Typical Derbyshire stone cottages nestle in the hollow at this waters meet.

An open lane
runs beside the
river in Bradford
Dale, seen here
where it rounds
a limestone cliff.

A packhorse track crosses the river beneath a small cliff.

This ancient track drops steeply from Youlgreave to the bridge in the dale.

Youlgreave spills down into the dale and here is an even older type of river crossing, a simple clapper bridge.

A second clapper bridge crosses
the river where it emerges from
the trees in its upper reaches.

The quiet wooded stretches of the river where it has been dammed to create fishponds.

A footpath crosses a dam and climbs to the road where a right turn leads into Youlgreave. Here the mullioned windows of the Old Hall have looked across the road since 1650.

Cyclists pause beside the circular conduit, oddly named The Fountain.

Ahead the church of All Saints'
seems to block the main street
through the village.

A backward look down the village street from the churchyard.

As at Fenny Bentley in the first walk, the church is well worth a visit. The massive Norman gritstone font has a holy water stoup seemingly held in the mouth of a strange creature. It is thought to be unique in England.

The alabaster effigy of Thomas Cockayne is of finer craftsmanship. It is only about 4ft long and one wonders why it is so small.

Continuing down the packhorse track into the dale we returned to the car, but turned down between the cottages to this delightful spot. Here we reminisced.

Postcript

Our minds went back over half a century to the 'Walk on a Spring Day' at the beginning of this book, and the intervening years spent in our glorious Derbyshire countryside. We have met many interesting and helpful people and made contact with others through my contributions to newspapers and magazines. Our friendship with Roy Christian extends over 36 years, during which time I have contributed photographs to his many books and articles to the national press while the series on Derbyshire Villages, in the *Derbyshire Life and Countryside*, now over 150 in number, is in preparation in book form with Breedon Books. My own series 'Derbyshire on Foot' has run to over 80 walks, 31 of which are included in *The Peak District on Foot* published by the *Derbyshire Countryside*. Many of the physical changes in the county are recorded in this book, also in my *Derbyshire Old and New*, but most staggering change is the enormous influx of visitors, with no less than 22 million coming into the county every year. Today walking is so popular that footpaths have been widened and often gravelled as in Dovedale where it can be almost crowded at times – so very, very different from that spring day in 1939!